Decide every day to be positive.

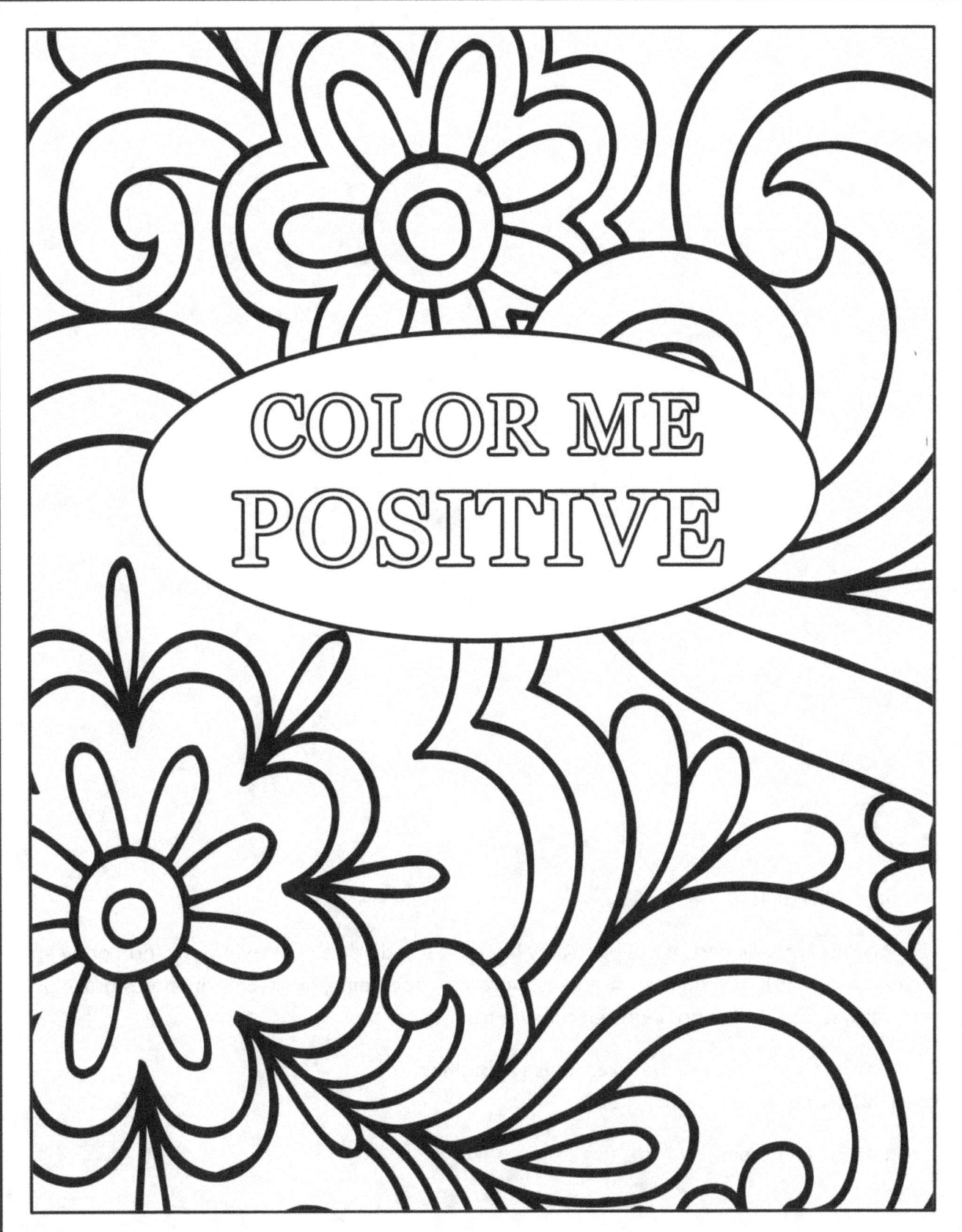

Published by Great Oaks Press/Parker House Publishing
www.ParkerHouseBooks.com

www.PositiveTribe.com

Color Me Positive *Coloring Book* is a collection of coloring pages embedded with positive messages. As you are coloring, your subconscious is taking in the positive message and in turn you may experience a more positive attitude.

Coloring gently helps you to de-stress from the day and allows you to release negative thoughts by focusing your mind on the present moment. The growing trend of grown-up coloring books is fast becoming one of the most popular ways to relax.

Featuring:

- 26 positive designs

- A variety of coloring designs meant to evoke peace and positivity.

- Images are on one side only to protect the designs under it and to be able to remove your beautifully colored positive message and frame it.

- Simple to complex designs for your every mood.

Directions: Use color pencils, crayons, gel pens or other coloring media to color the designs. If using a wet media like markers or paint, place a piece of paper under the design you are coloring to protect the next design. There is no right or wrong way to use this book because it is always right!

Peace ~ Love ~ Color!

Candi Parker

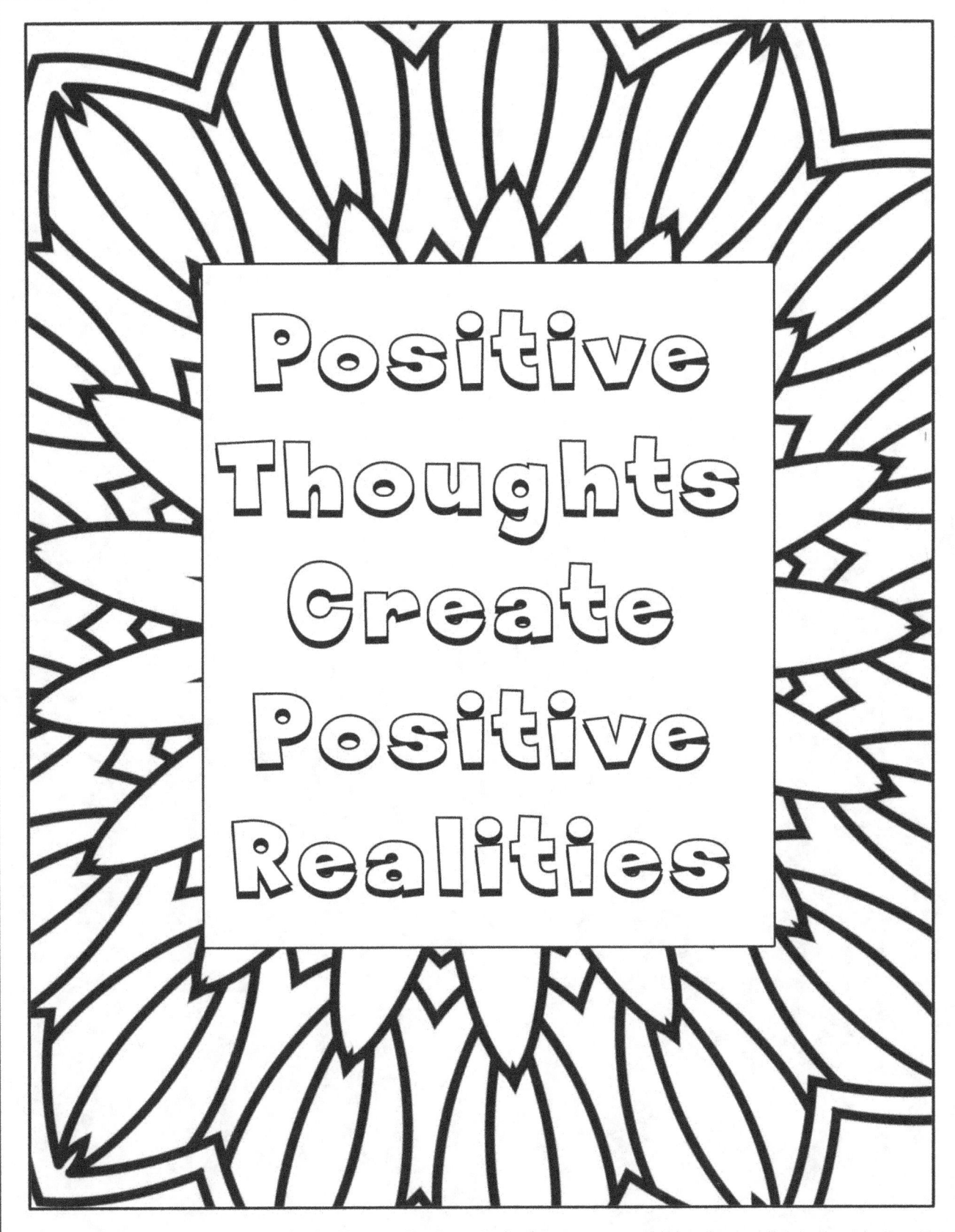

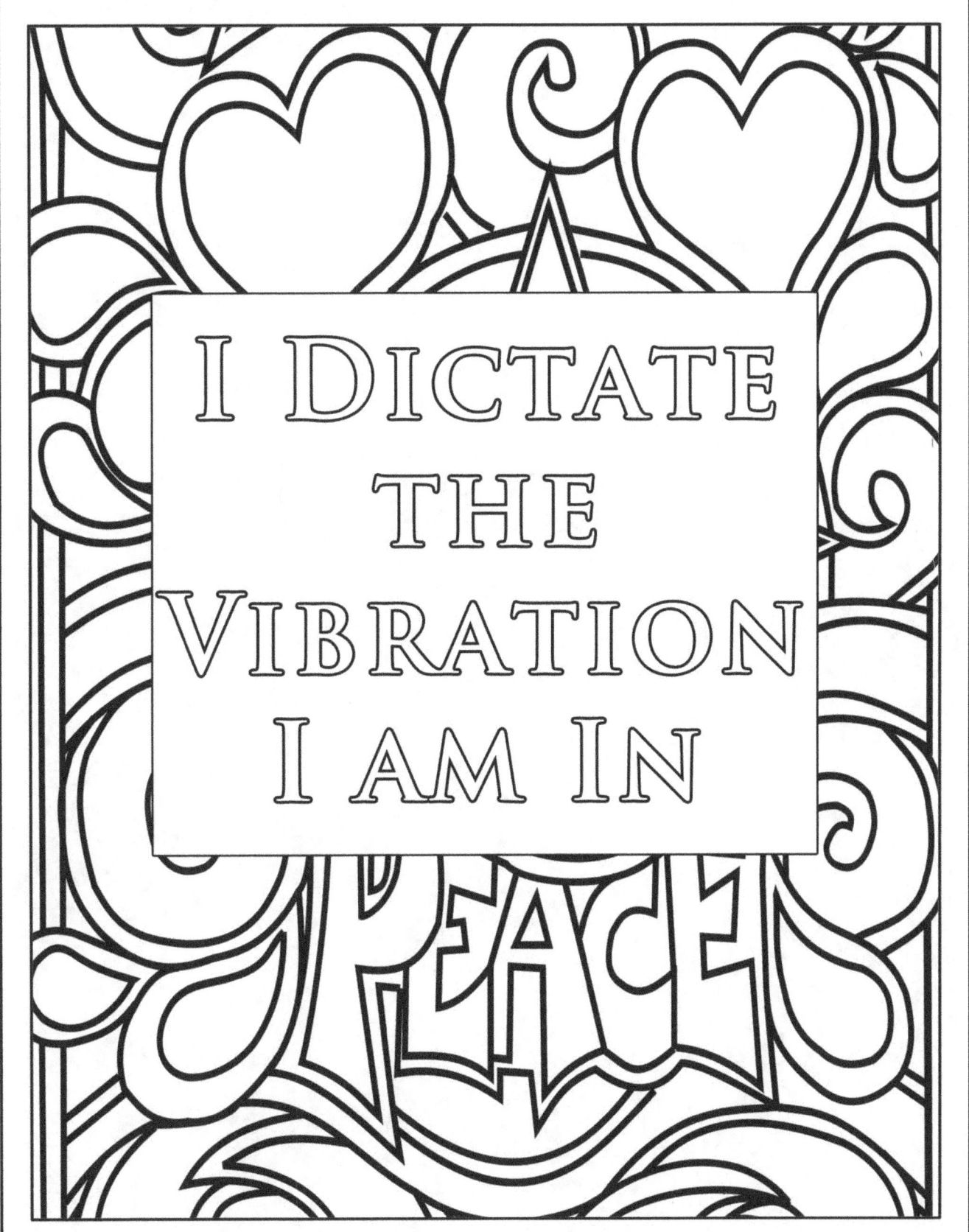

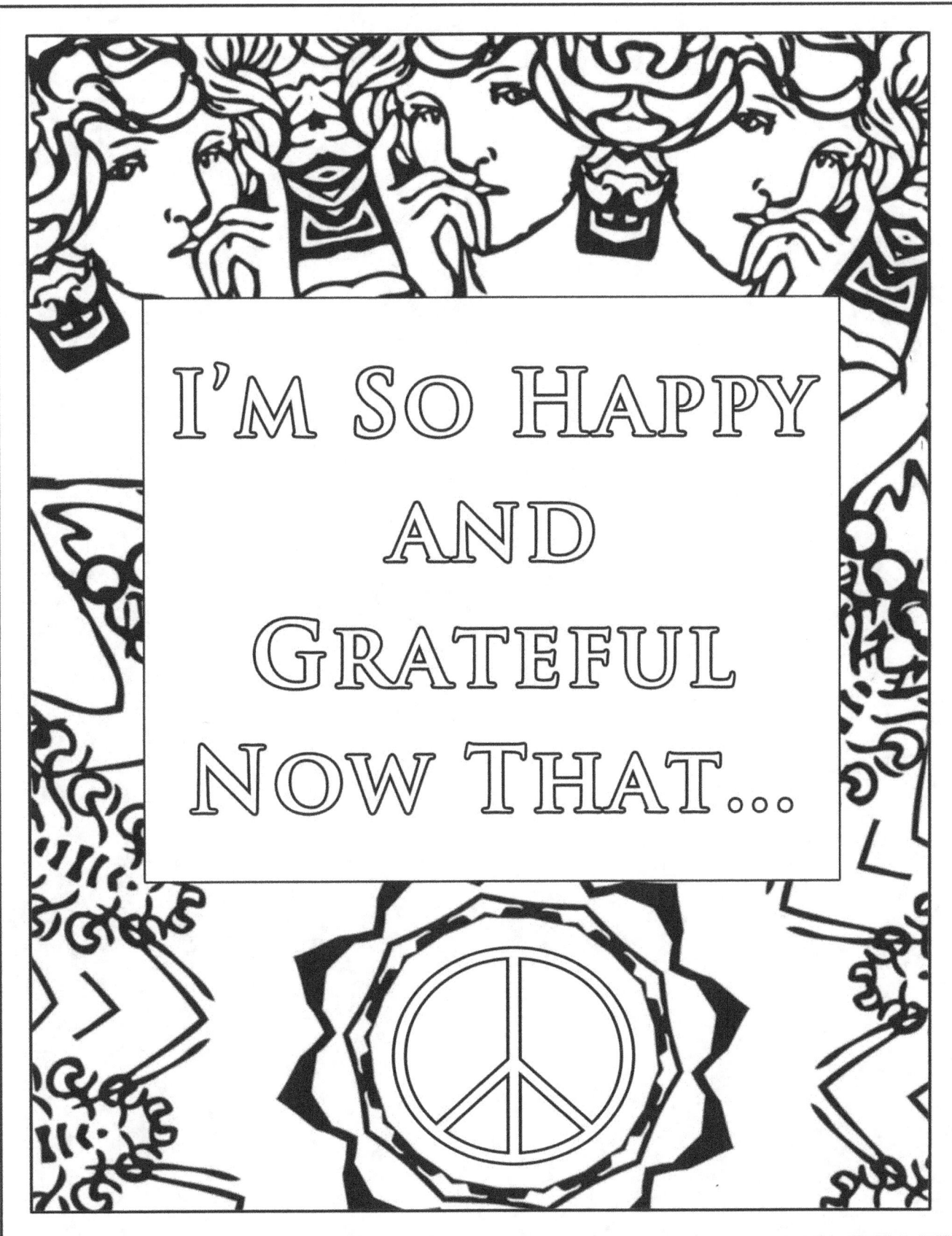

I'M SO HAPPY AND GRATEFUL NOW THAT...

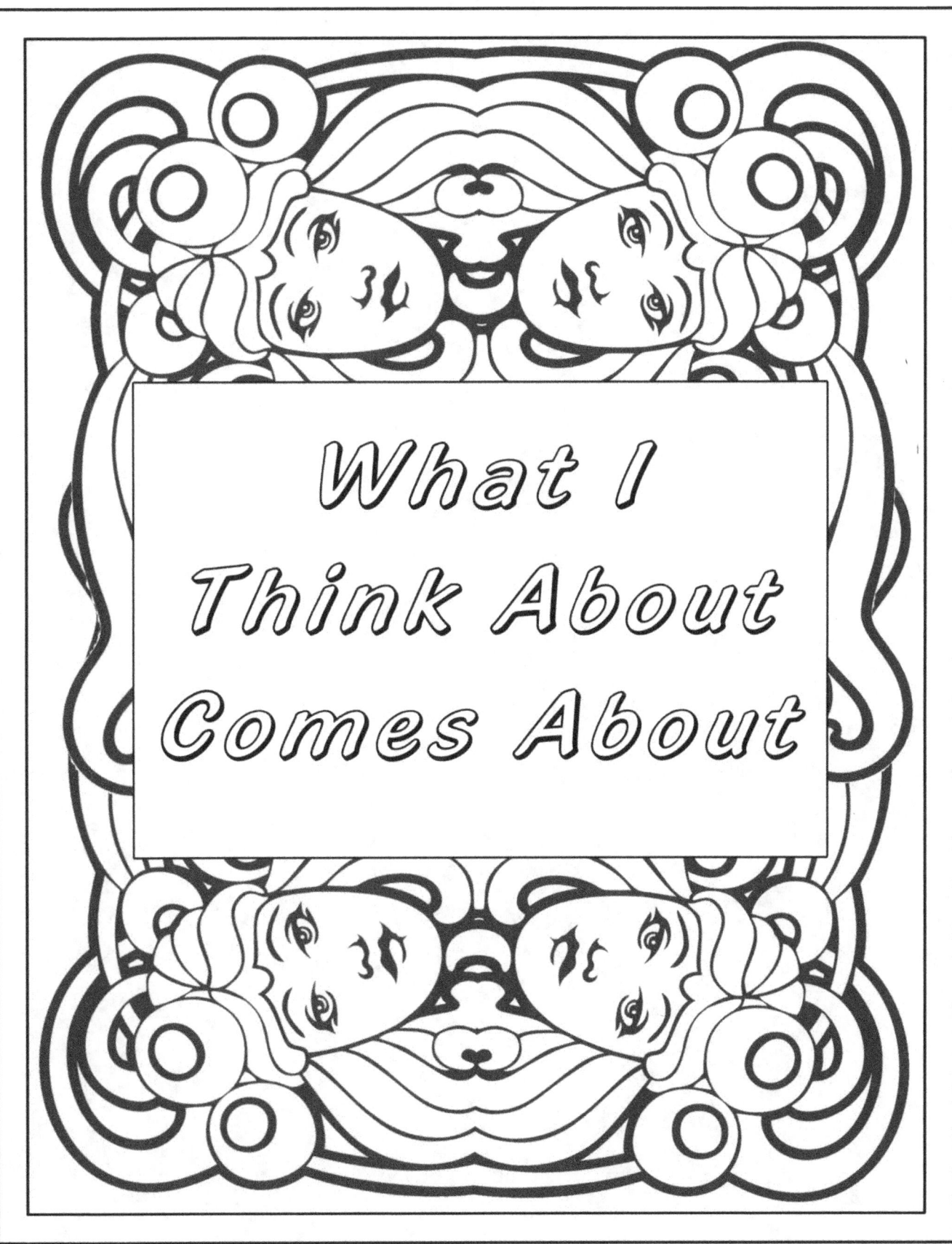

What I
Think About
Comes About

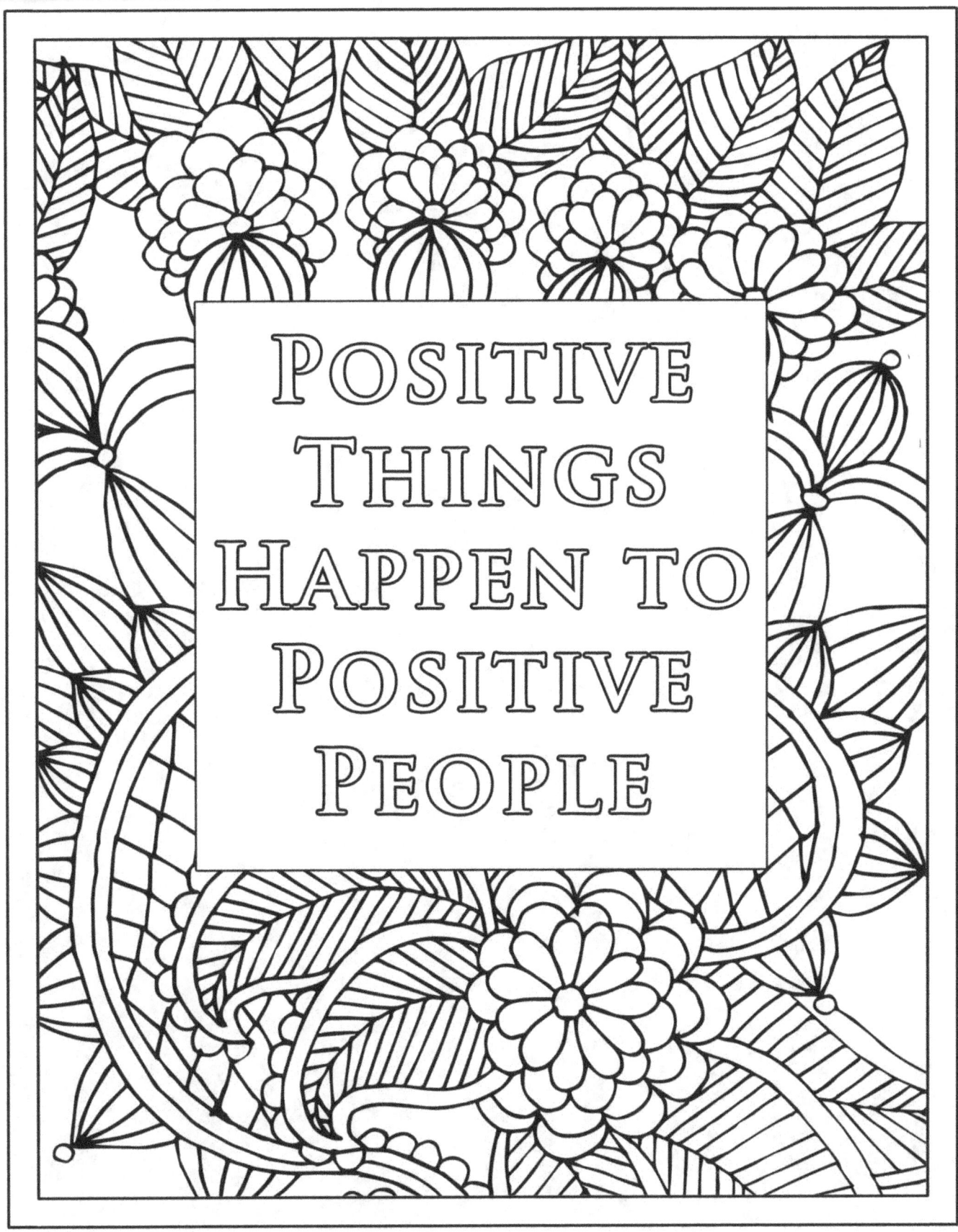

POSITIVE THINGS HAPPEN TO POSITIVE PEOPLE

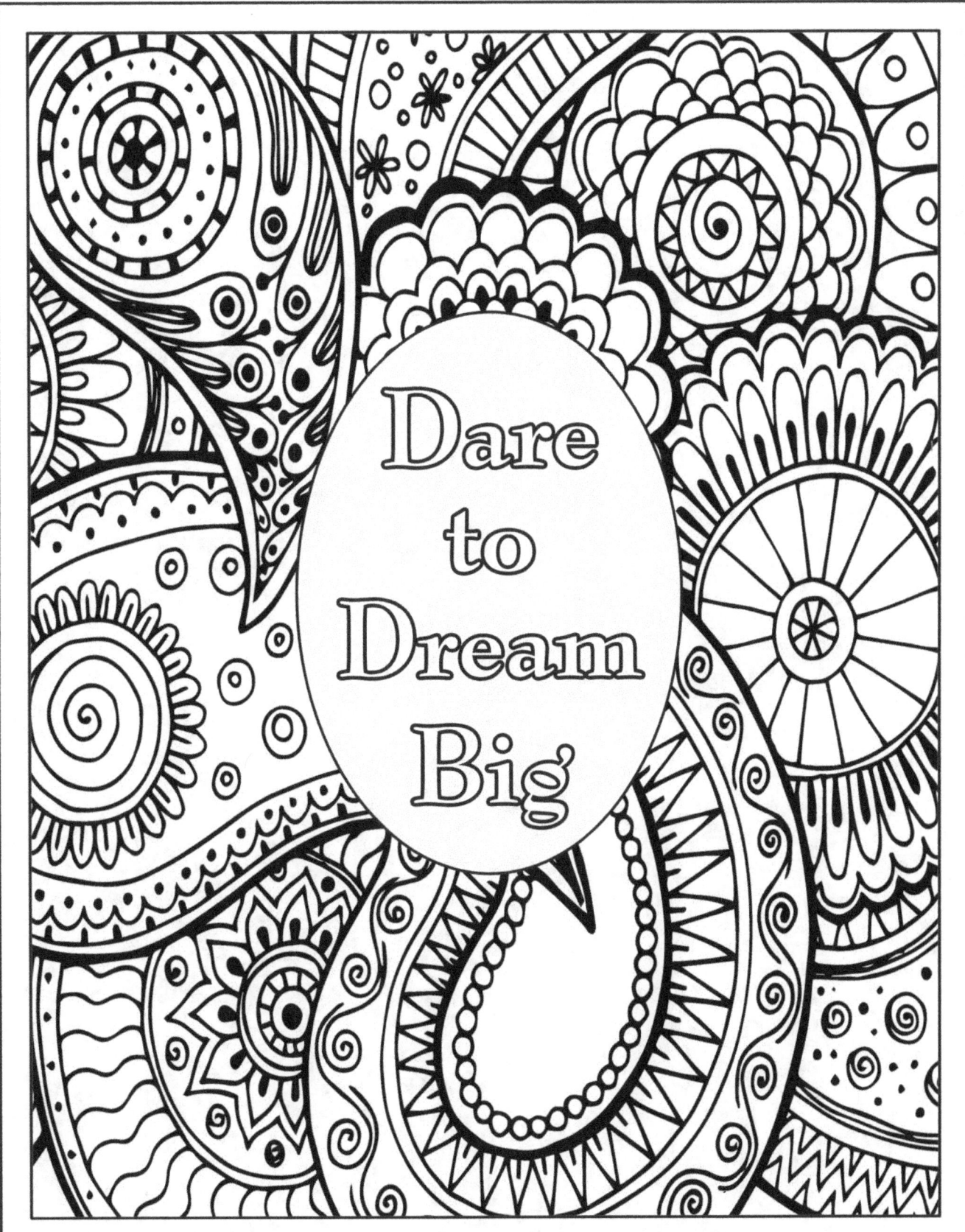

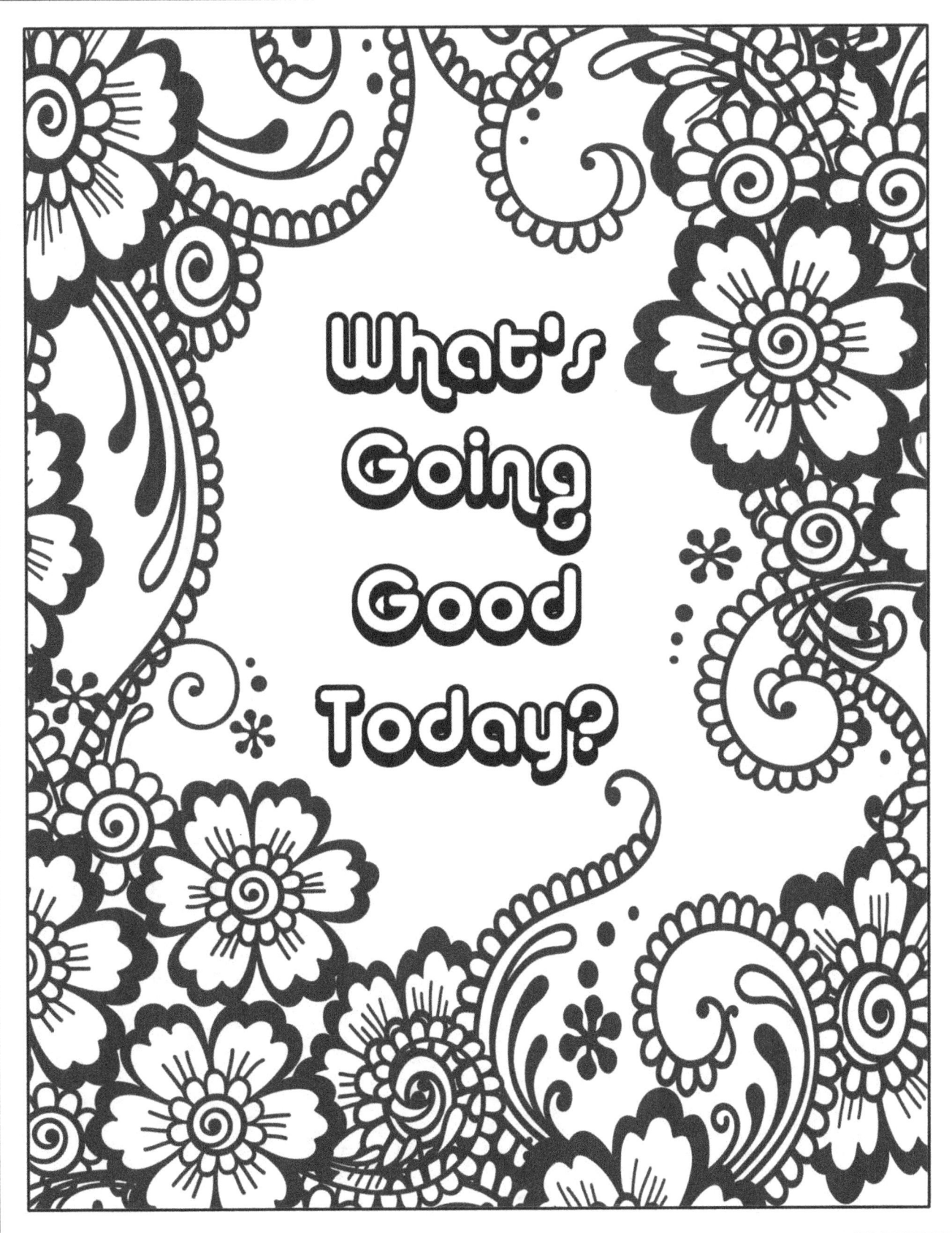

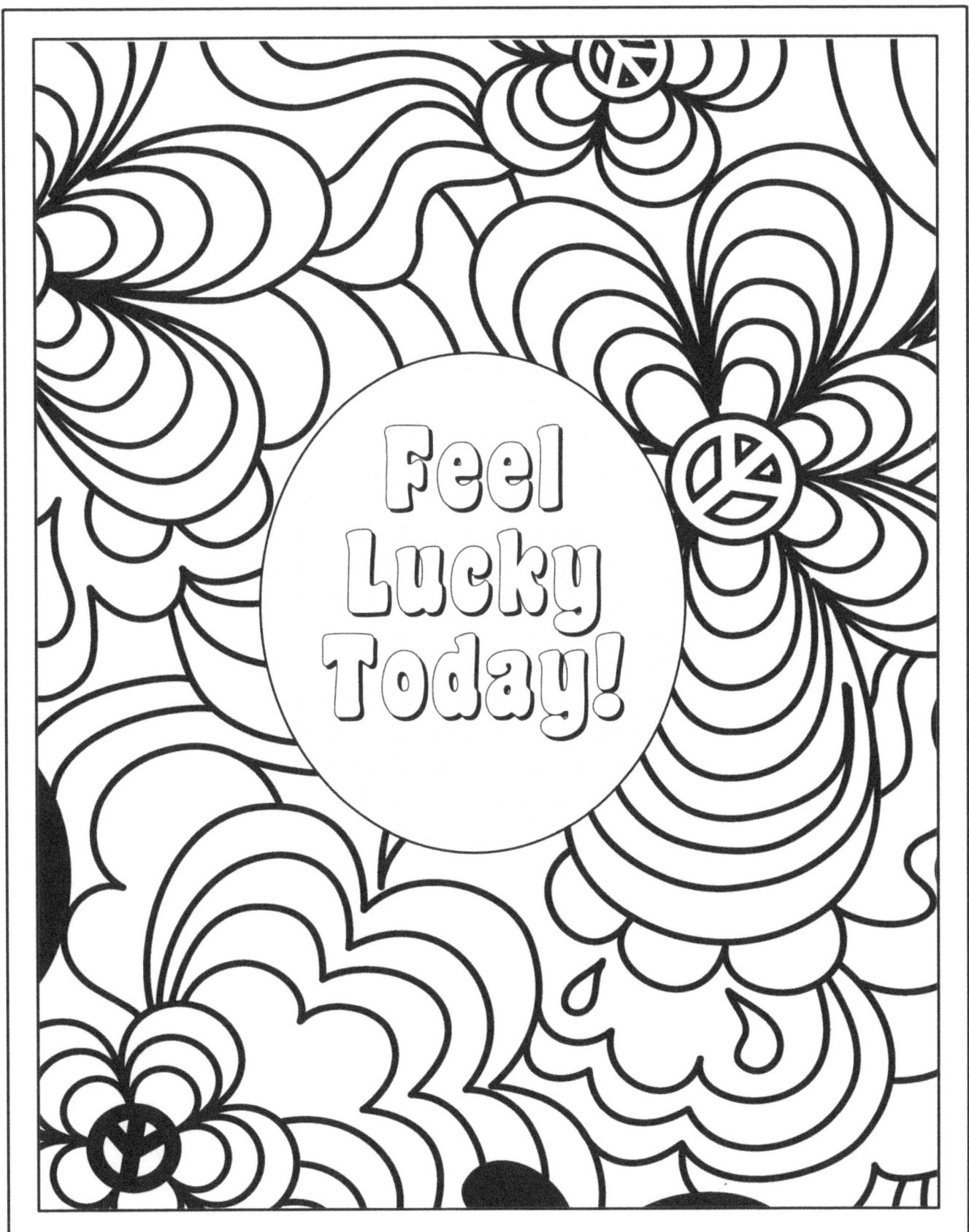

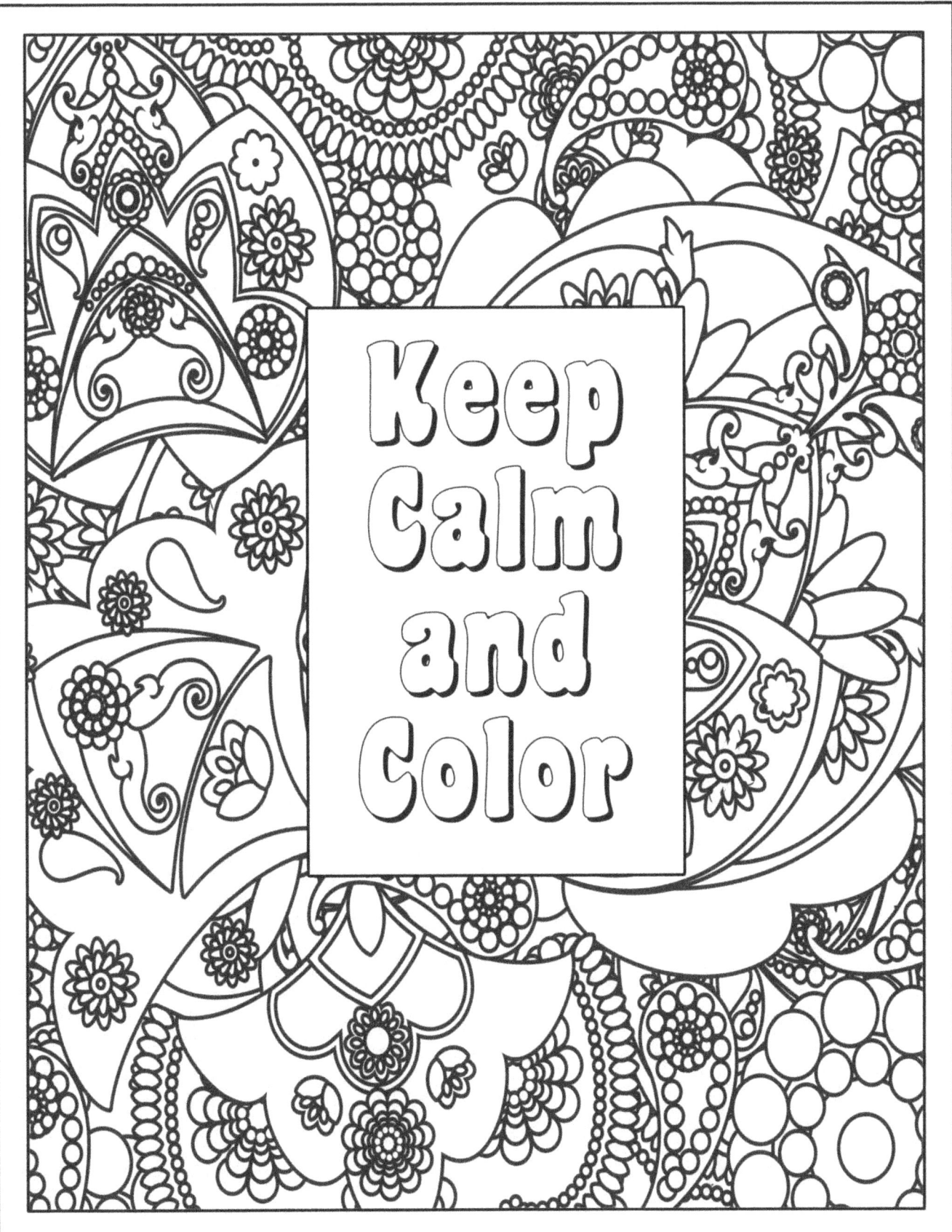

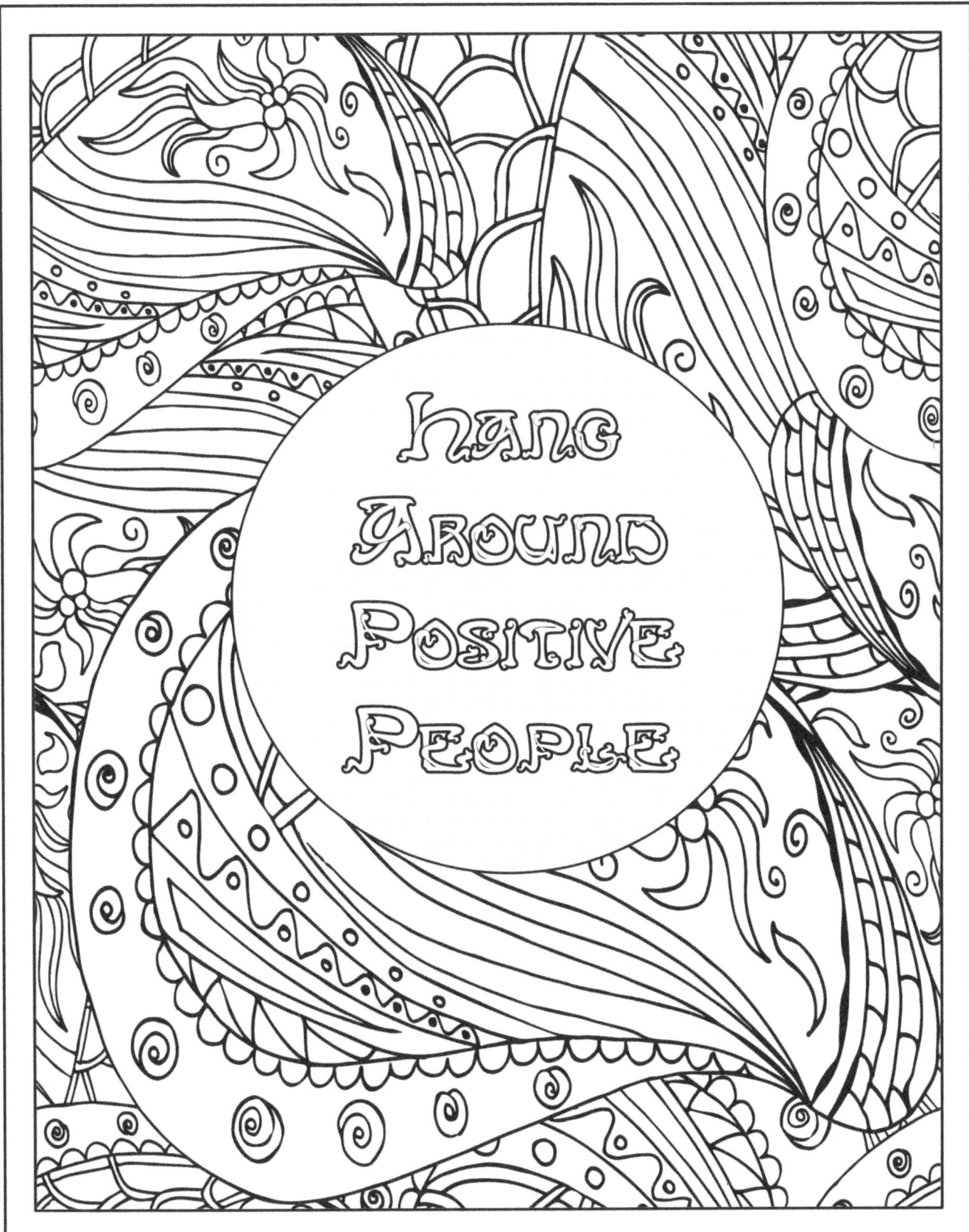

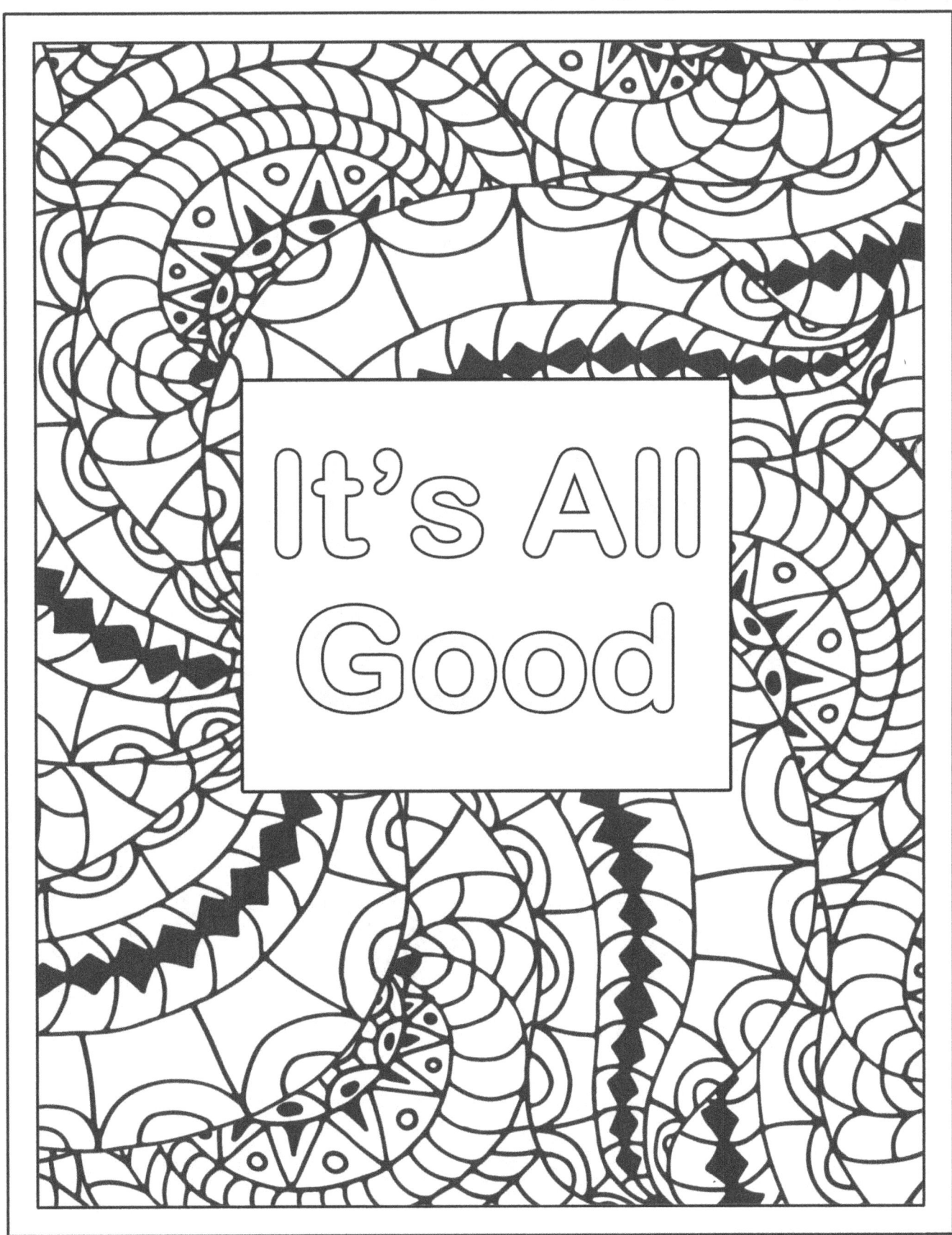

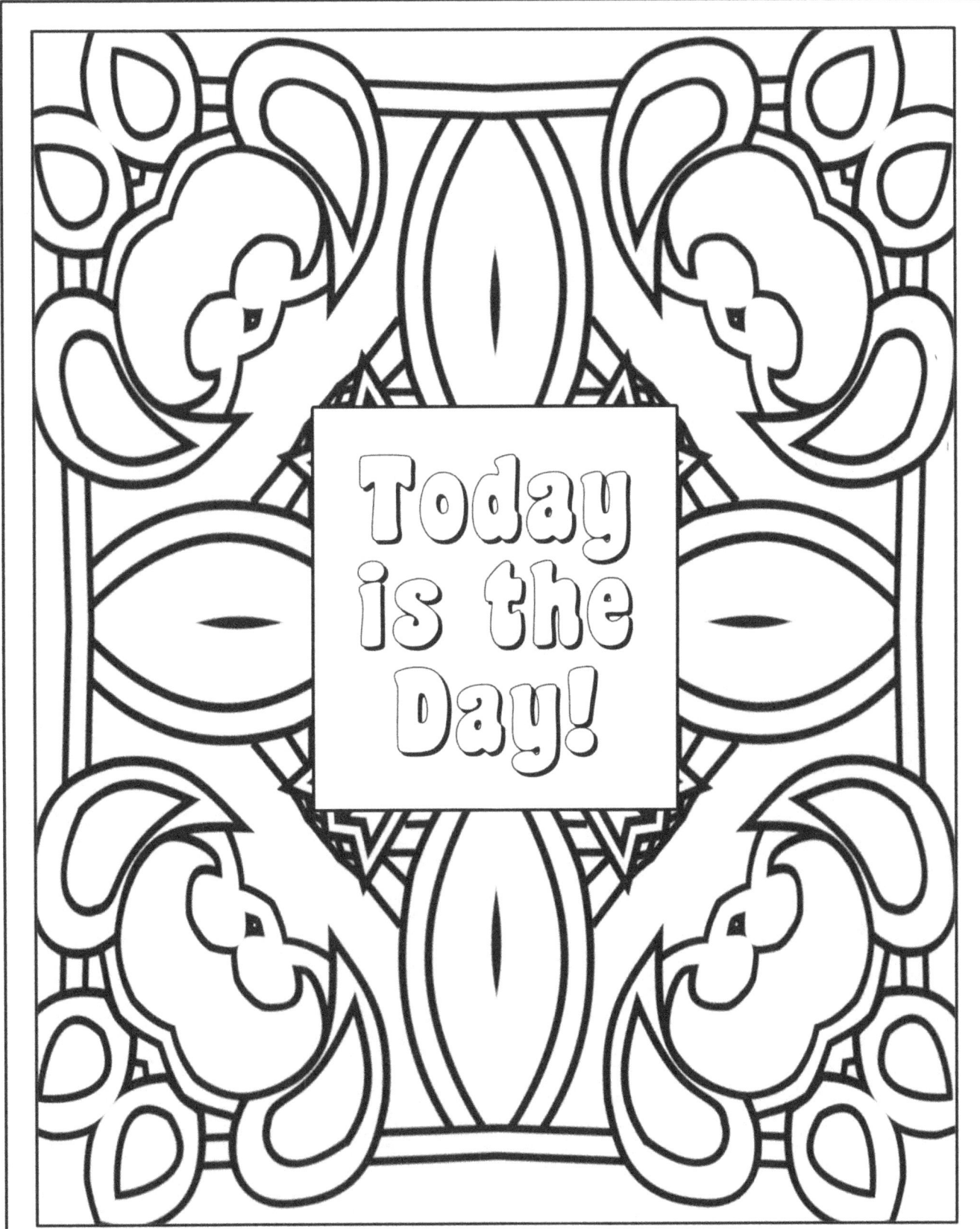

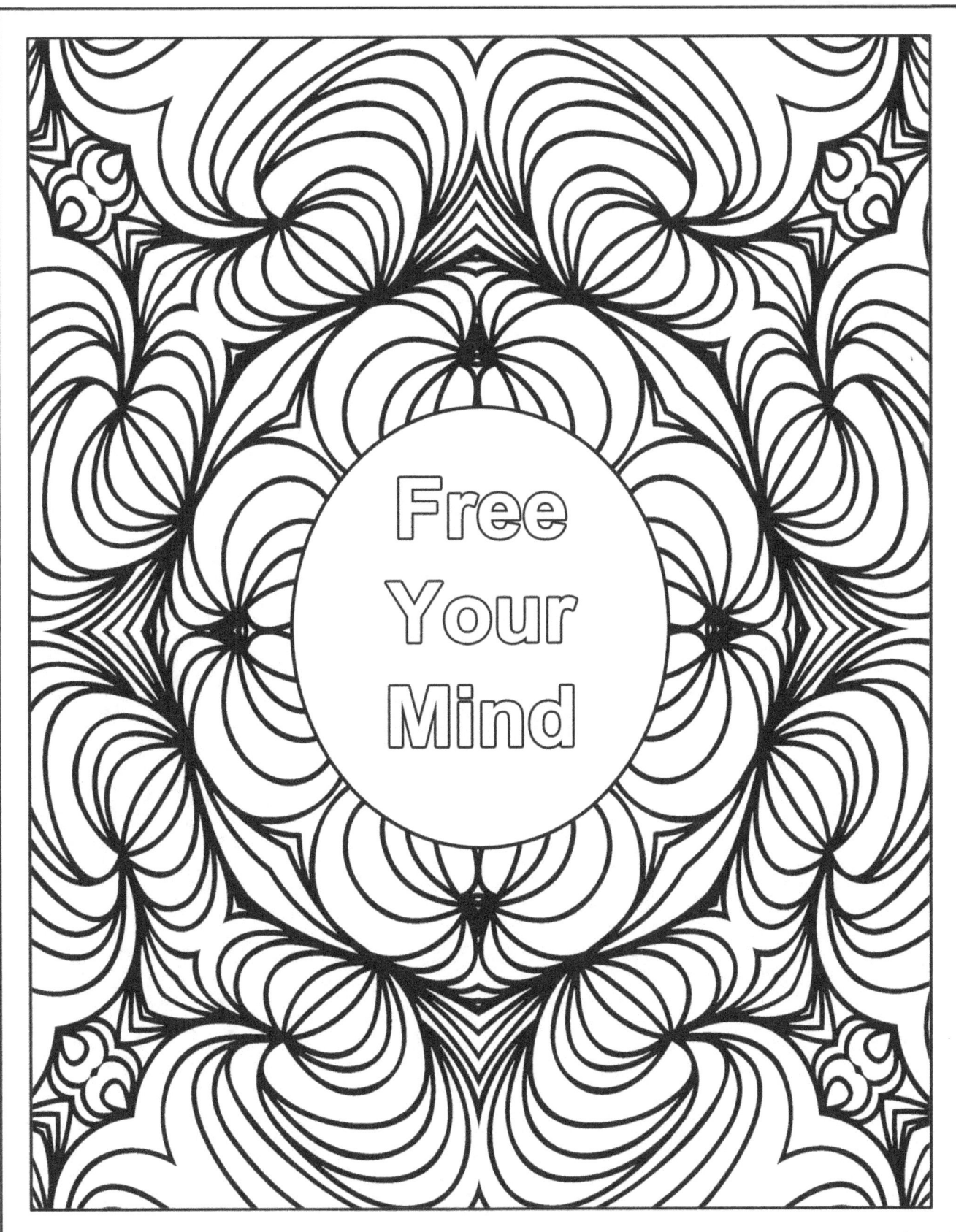

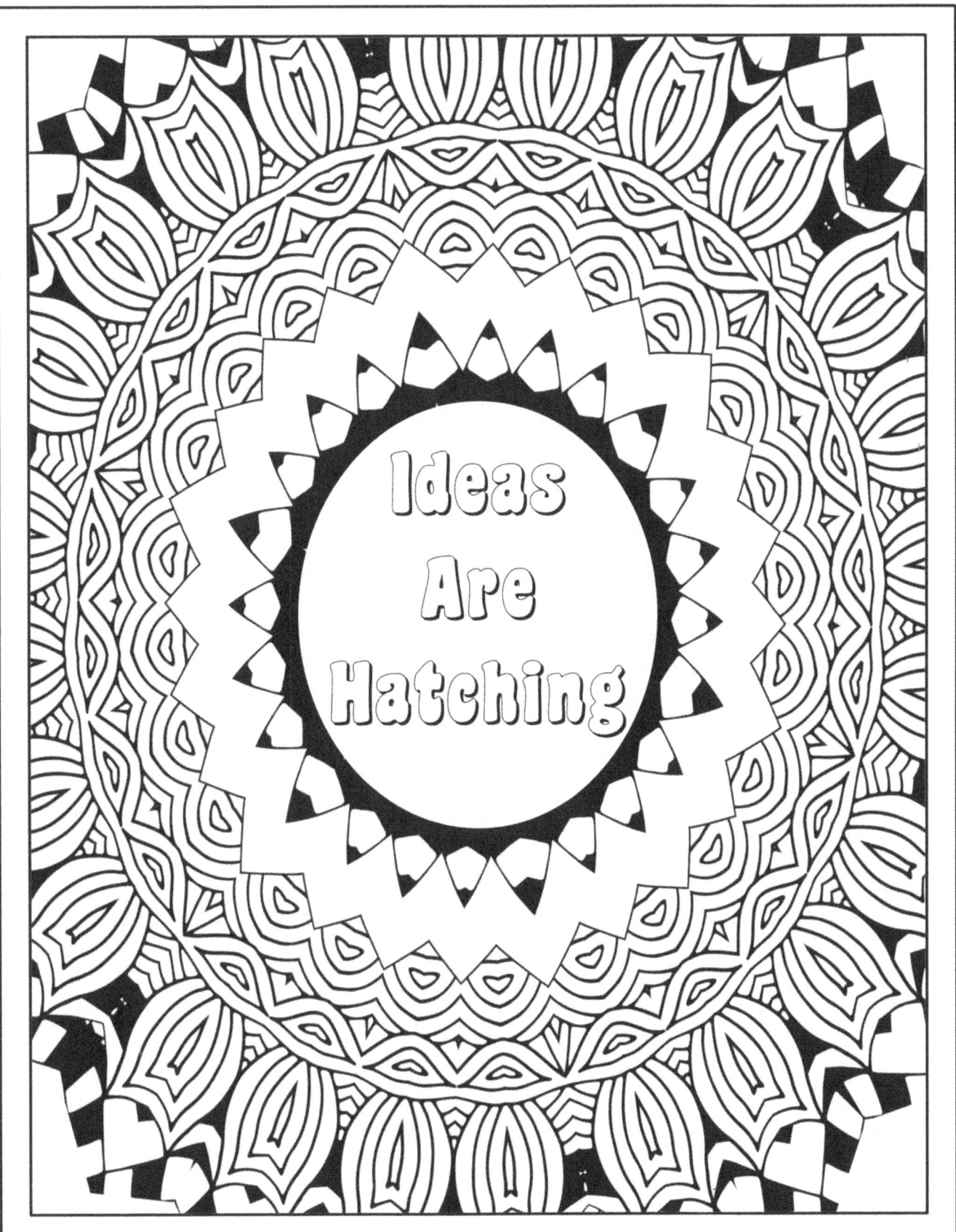

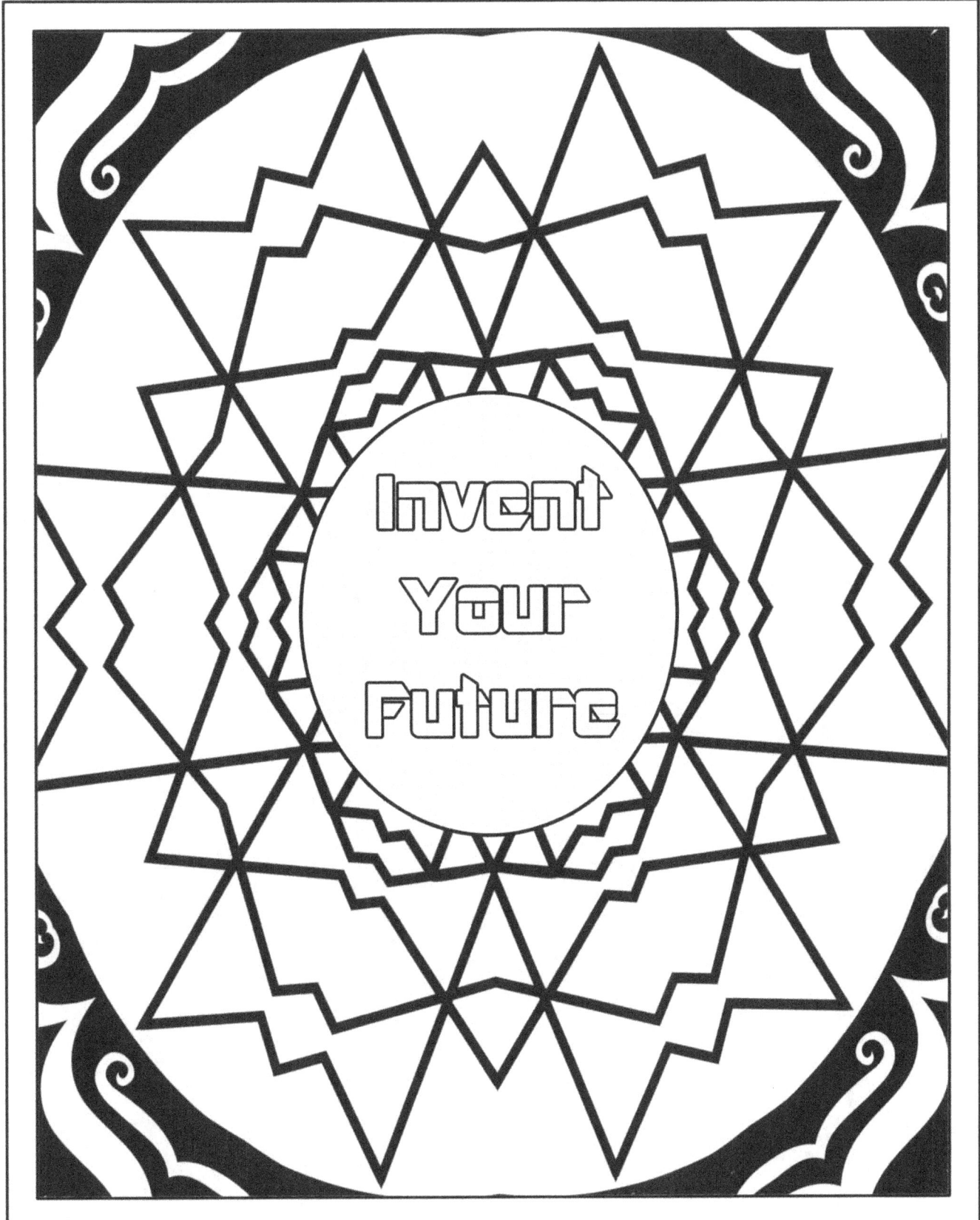

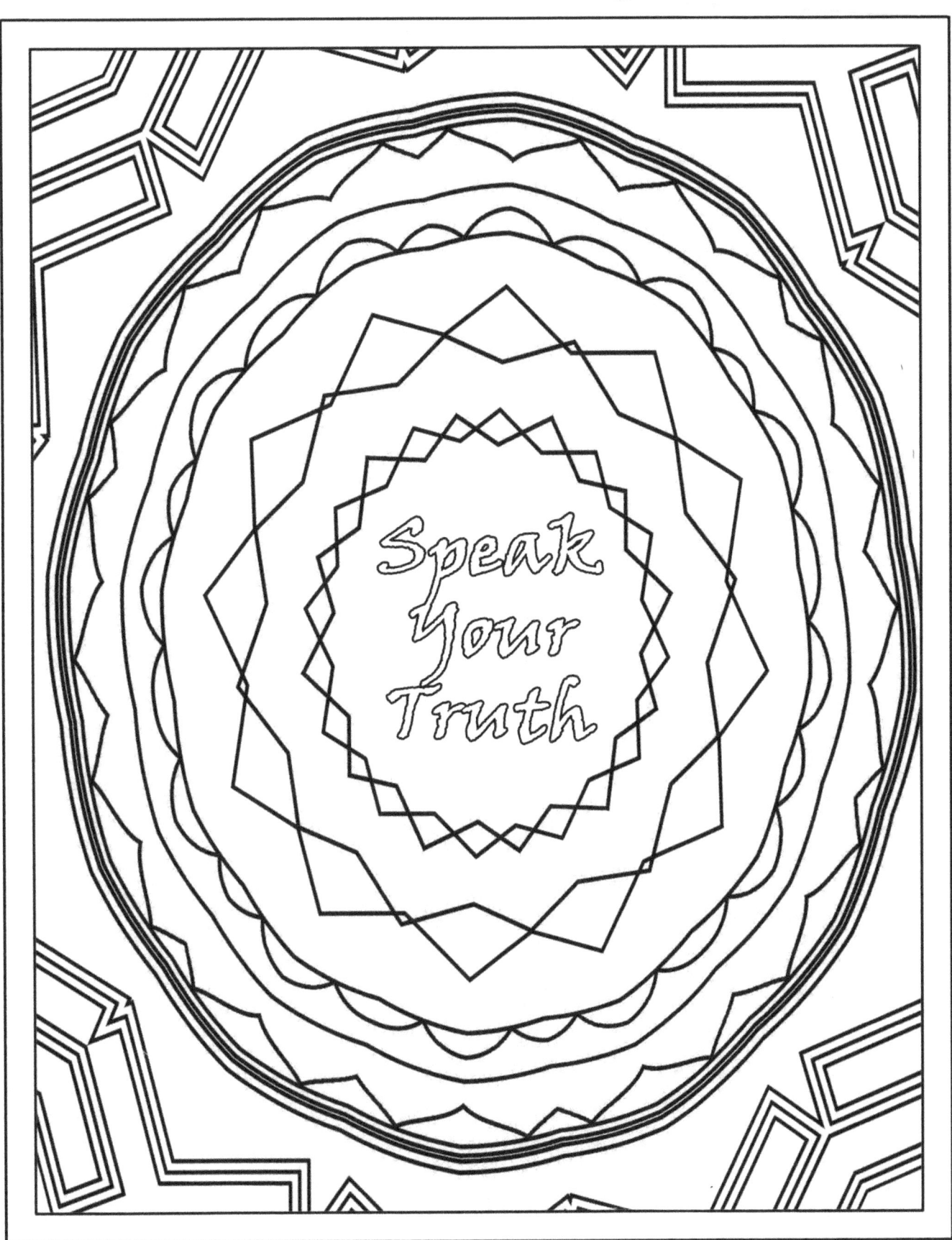

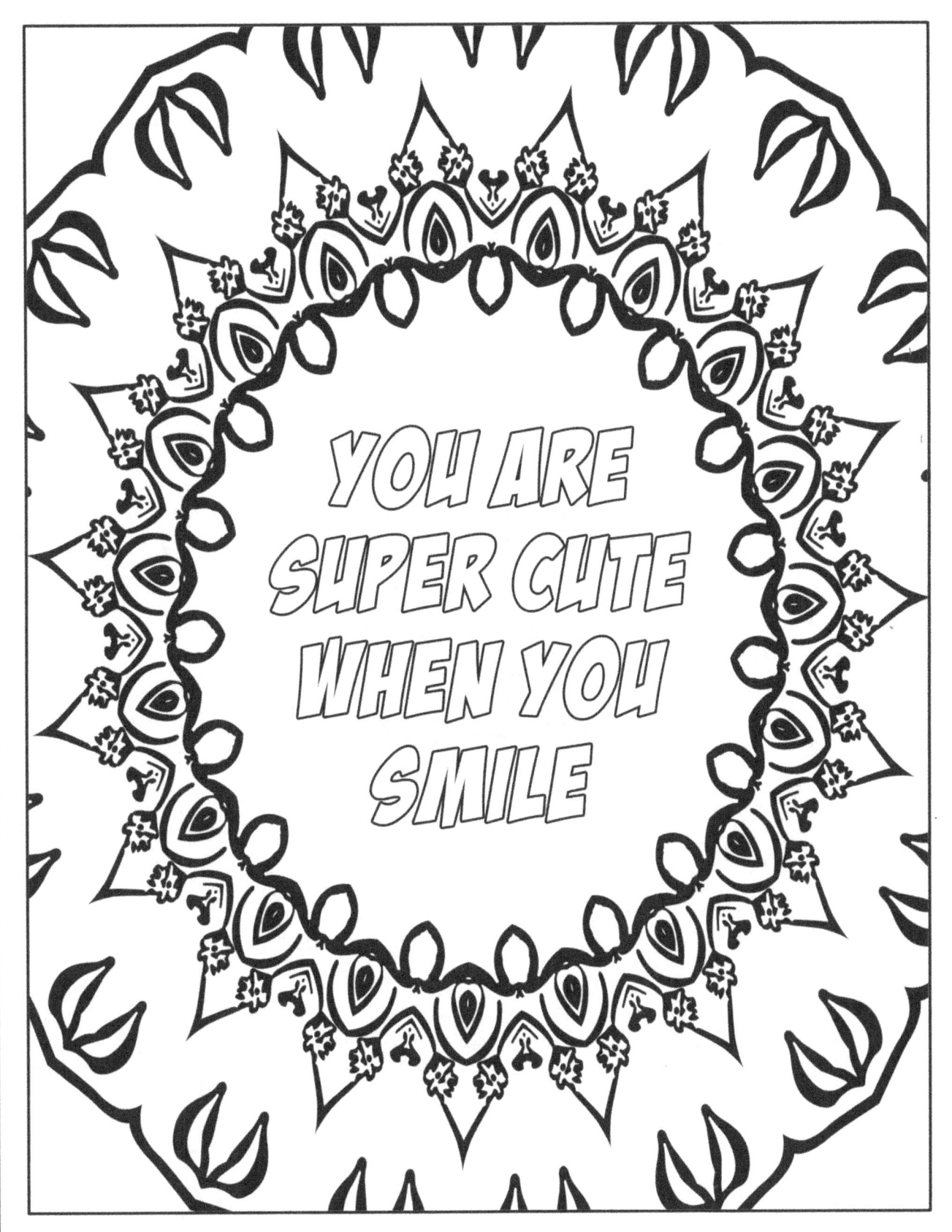

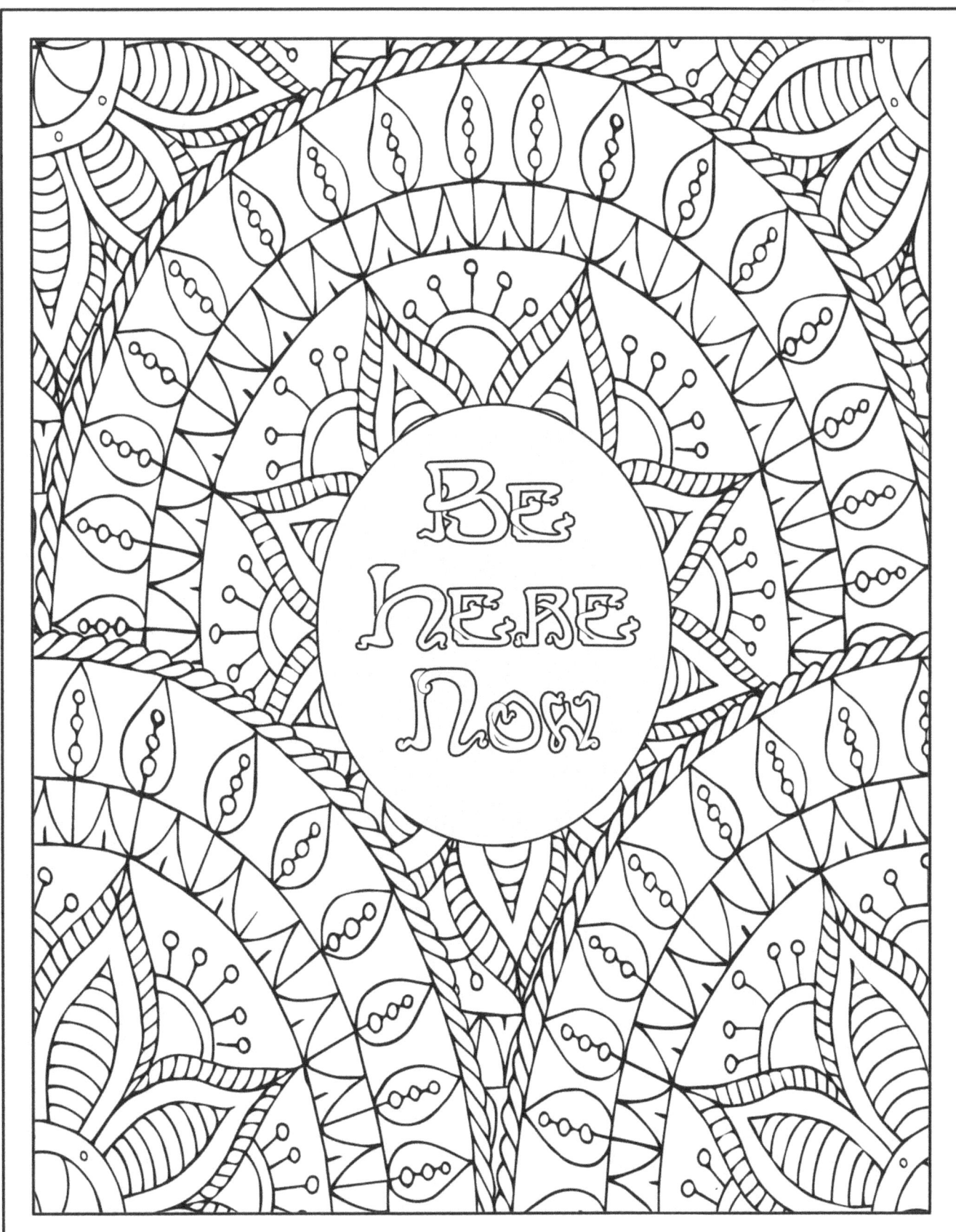

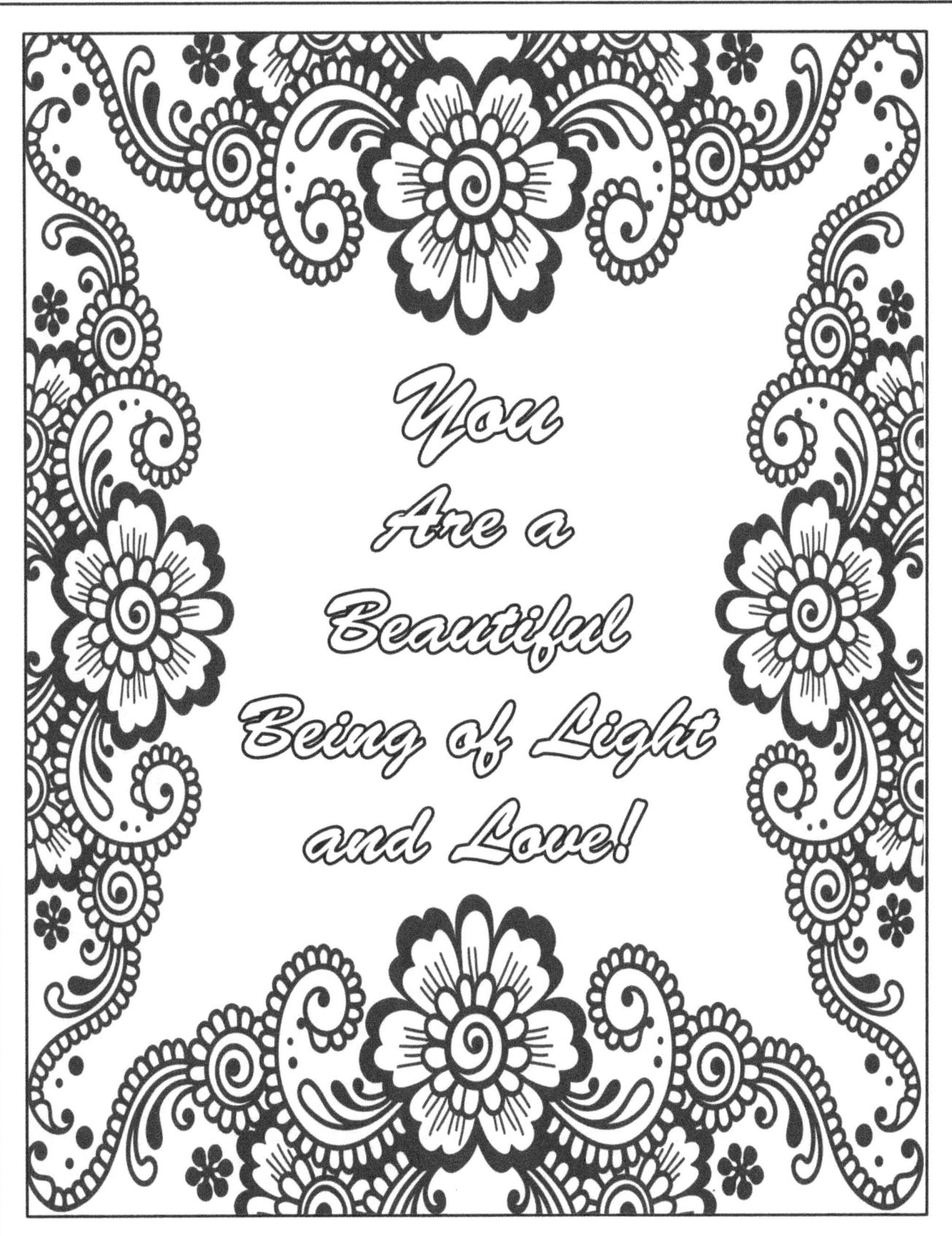

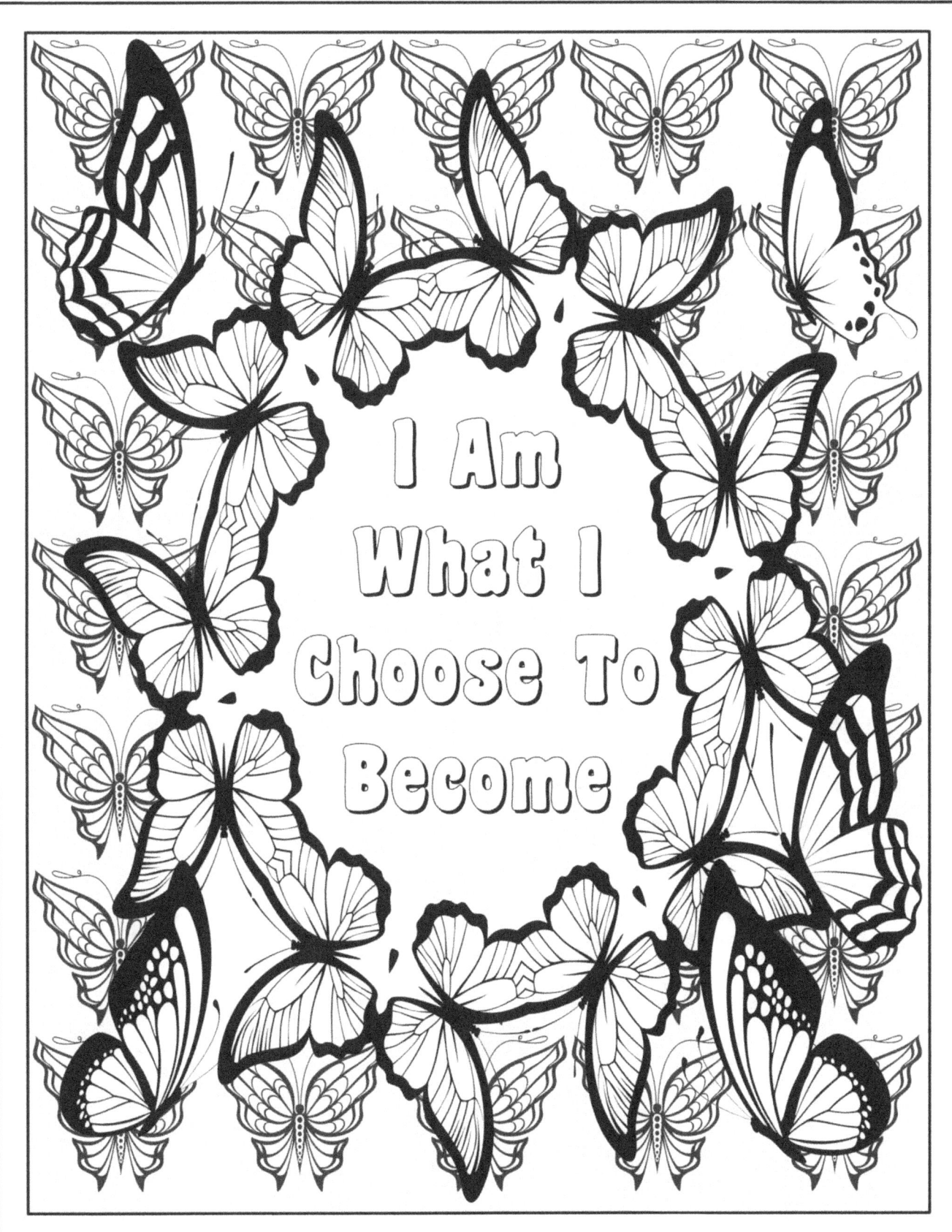

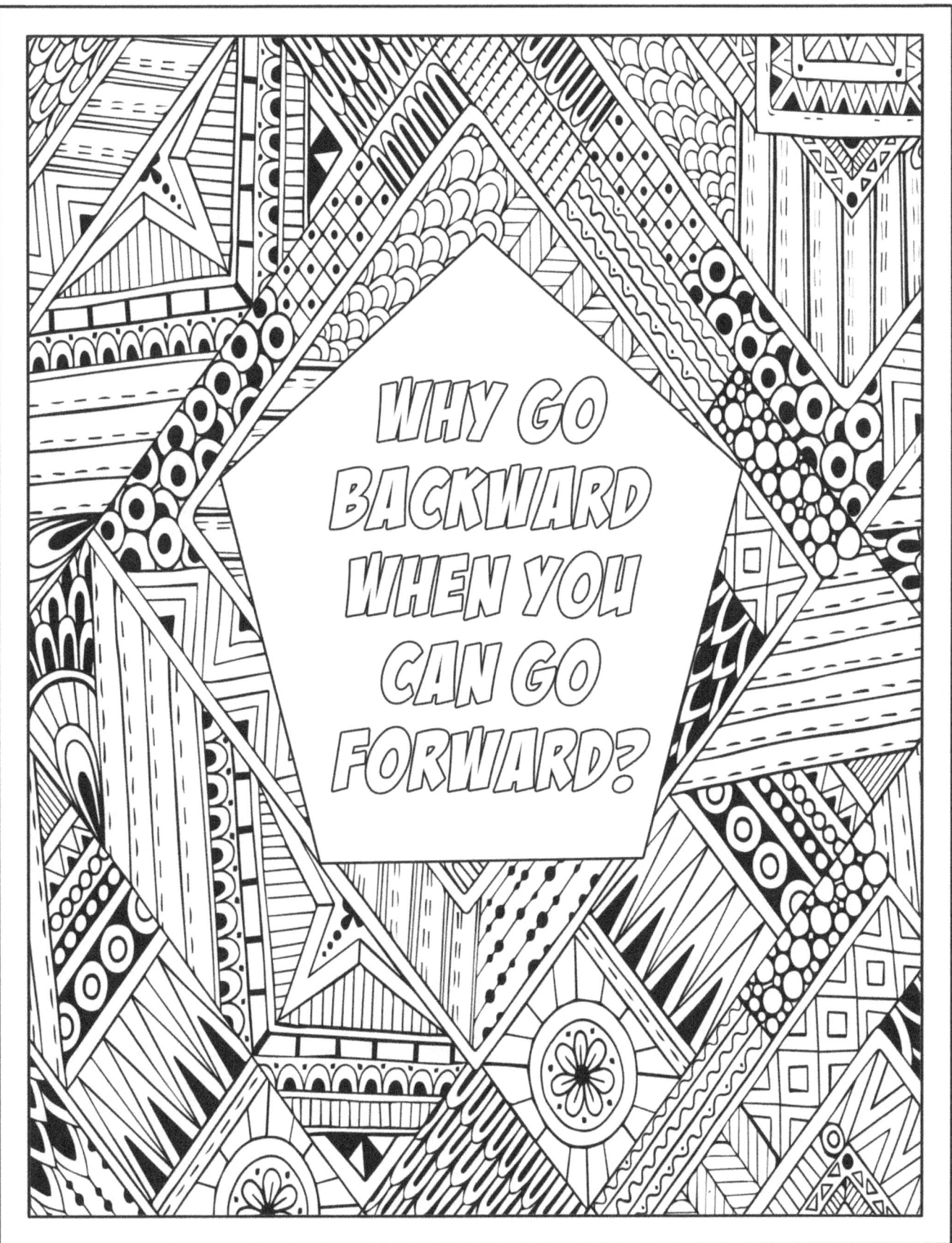

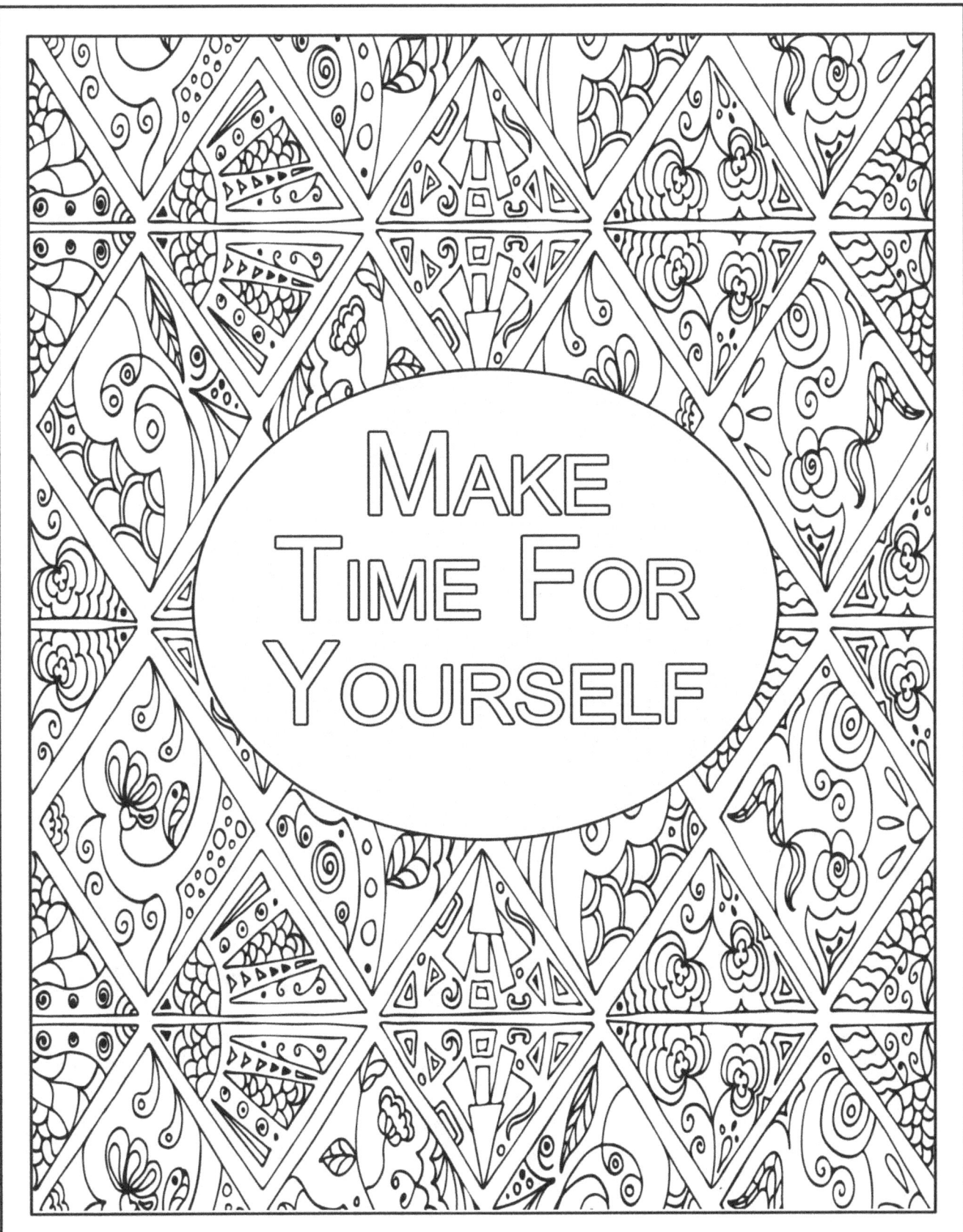

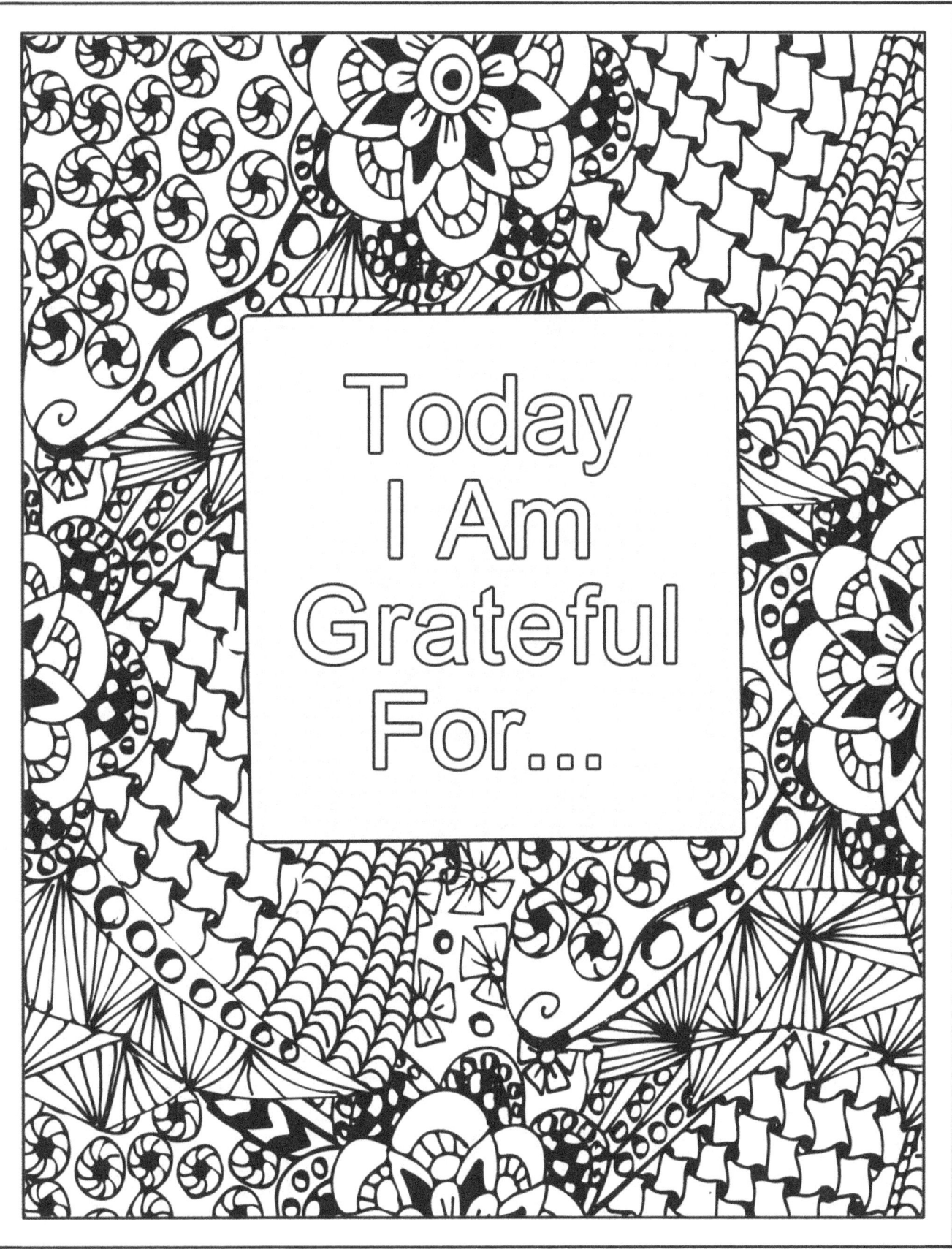

Today
I Am
Grateful
For...

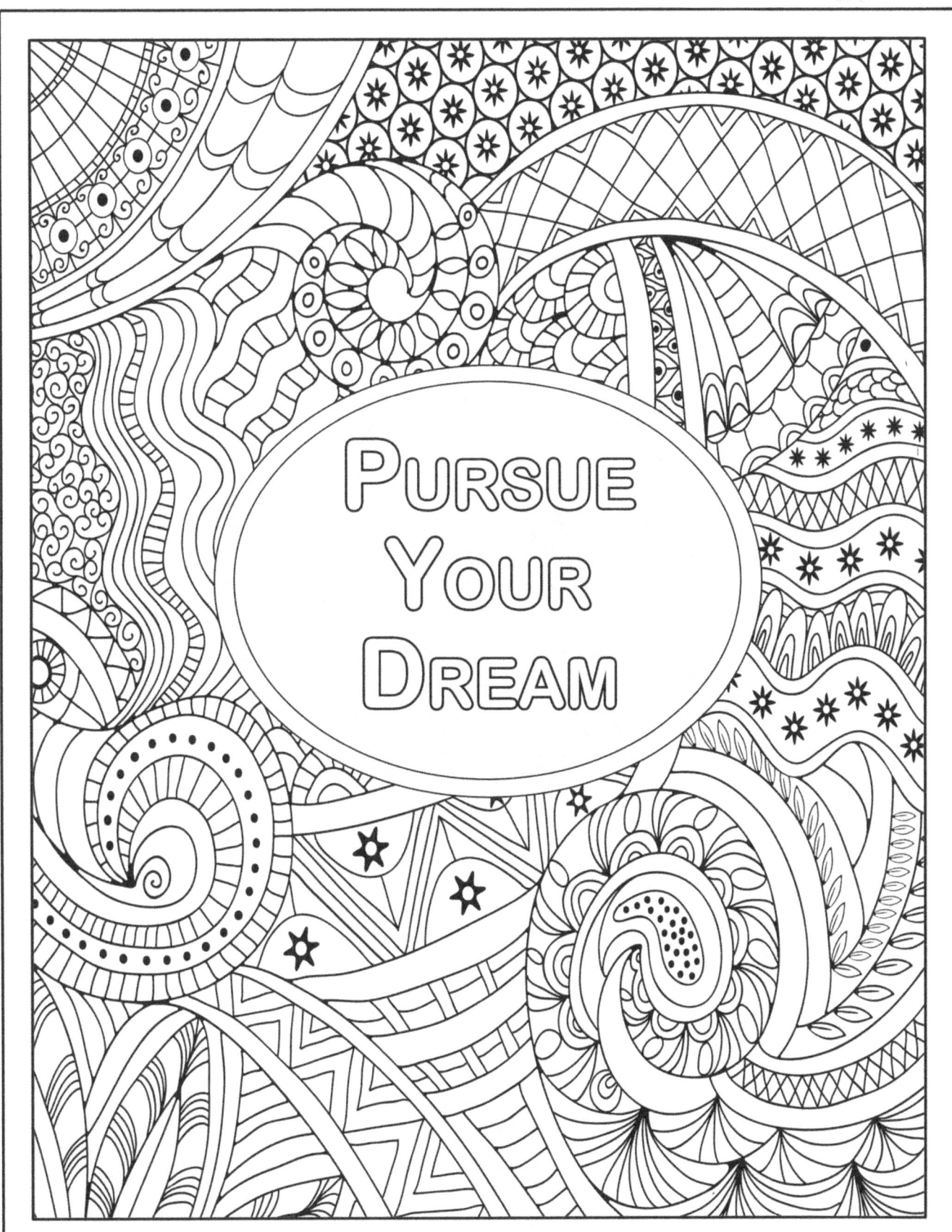

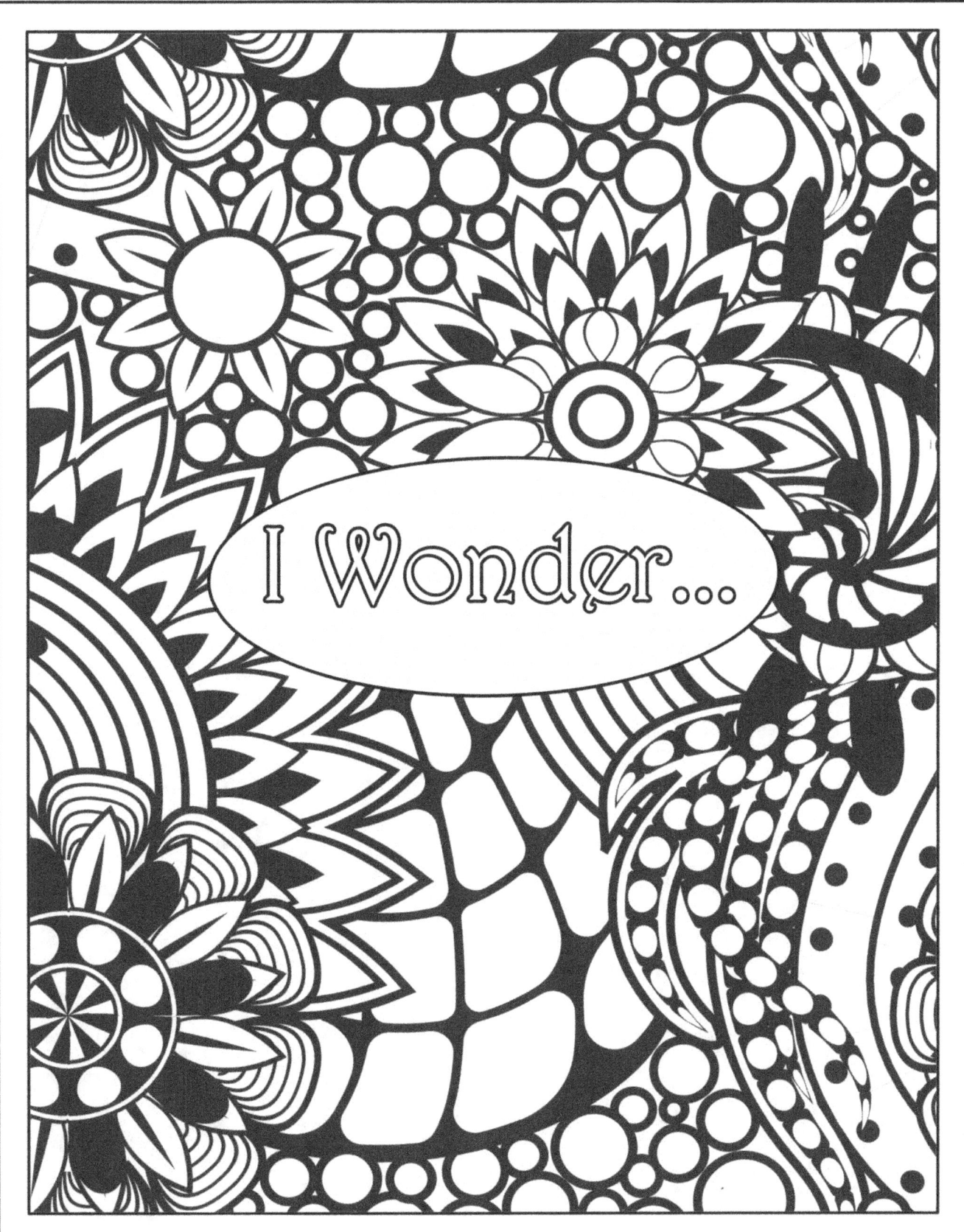

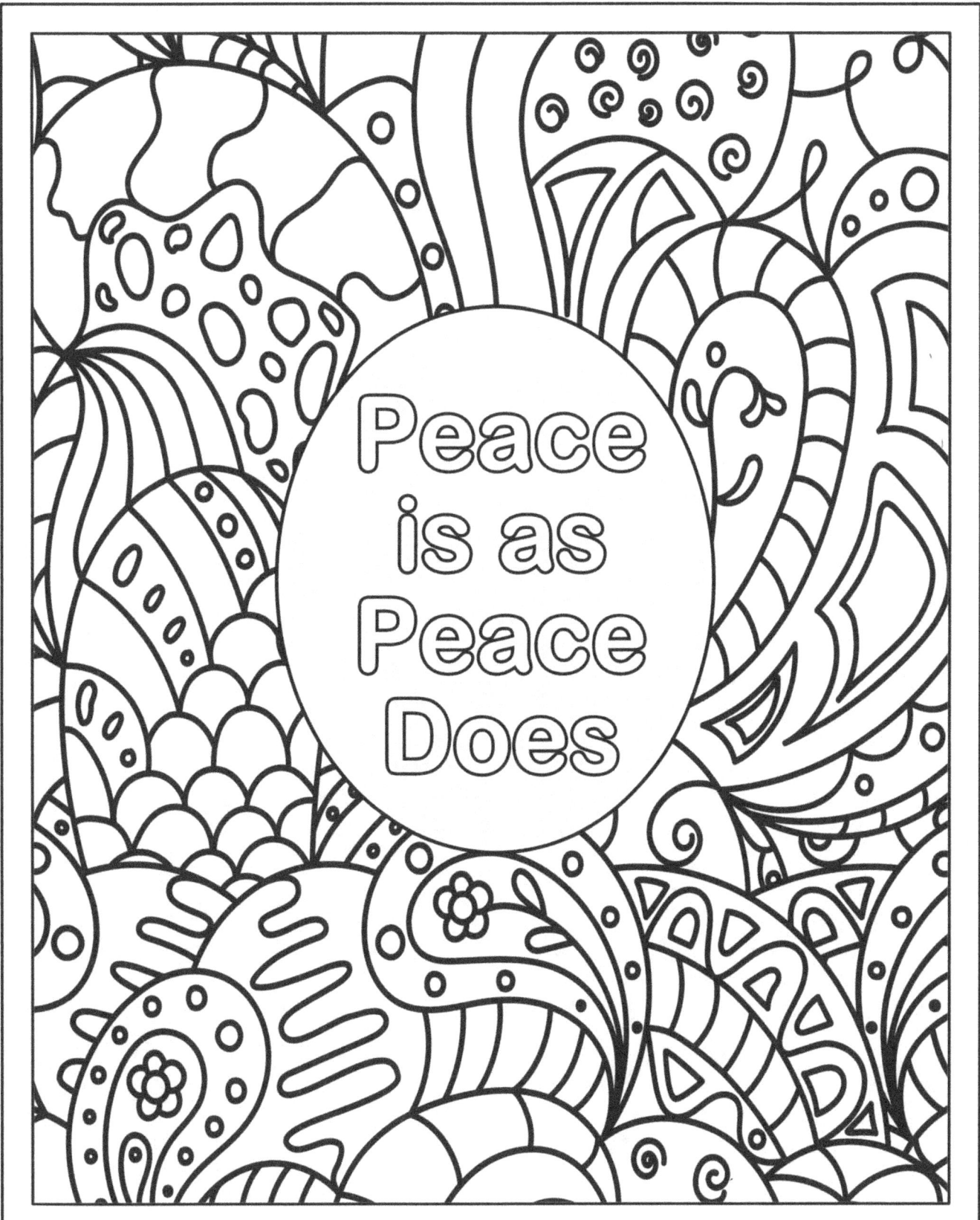

> A simple shifting of your emotions
> Can change your entire day!

Join the Positive Tribe community!

Facebook.com/PositiveTribe

Dedicated to a positive world!

If you liked this you may also like my other coloring book

Happy Hippy Coloring Book
For Hippies of All Ages

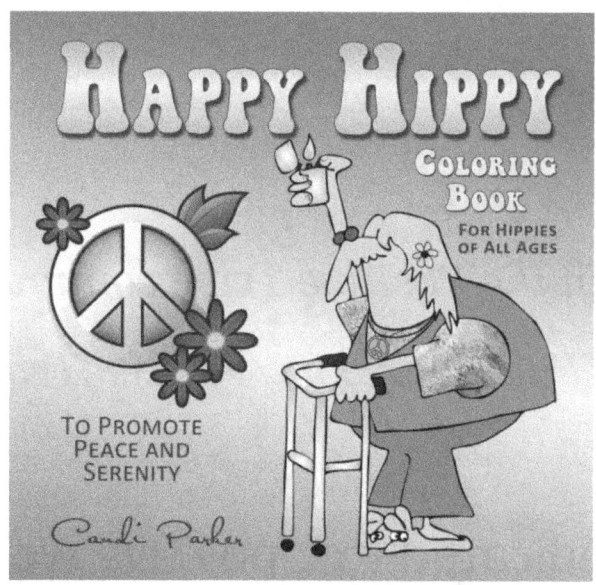

On Amazon.com and HappyHippyHome.com